Ellen Ochoa

By Elizabeth D. Jaffe

Consultant
Nanci R. Vargus, Ed.D.
Assistant Professor of Literacy
University of Indianapolis, Indianapolis, Indiana

New York   Sydney
                                Hong Kong
Danbury, Connecticut

Designer: Herman Adler Design
Photo Researcher: Caroline Anderson
The photo on the cover shows Ellen Ochoa.

Library of Congress Cataloging-in-Publication Data

Jaffe, Elizabeth Dana.
  Ellen Ochoa / by Elizabeth D. Jaffe.
    p. cm. – (A rookie biography)
  Includes bibliographical references and index.
  ISBN 0-516-21721-6 (Lib. Bdg.)   0-516-25827-3 (Pbk.)
  1. Ochoa, Ellen–Juvenile literature. 2. Women astronauts–United States–
Biography–Juvenile literature. 3. Astronauts–United States–Biography–
Juvenile literature. 4. Hispanic Americans in the professions–Juvenile literature.
5. Hispanic American women–Biography–Juvenile literature. I. Title. II. Series.
  TL789.85.O25J34 2004
  629.45'0092–dc22

                            2004000427

Where would you like to go in space?

4

Would you like to visit the
moon? Would you like to see
Earth from space?

You could if you were an
astronaut like Ellen Ochoa.

Ellen Ochoa was born on May 10, 1958. She was born in Los Angeles, California. She always wanted to be an astronaut.

8

Ellen worked hard in school.
She was a very good student.

She liked math and music.
She learned to play the flute.

In college, Ellen studied math and science. She went to college for many years.

She became an engineer. But, she still wanted to be an astronaut.

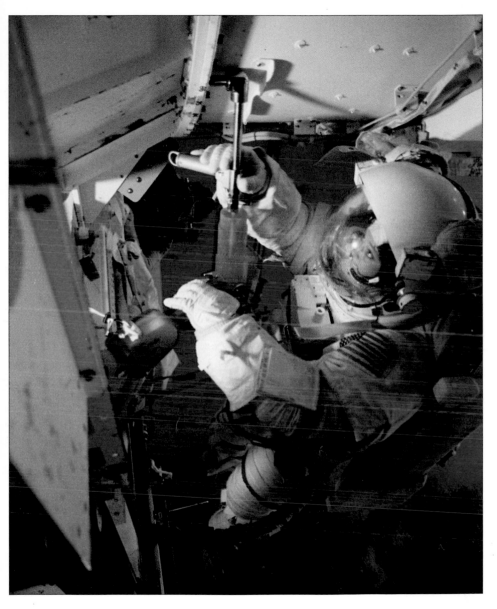

11

The United States government
was looking for astronauts.

Being an astronaut is hard
work. Astronauts must be
healthy. They must have a
good education, too.

Ellen Ochoa knew she could be a good astronaut. She asked to join the United States Astronaut Program. At first, the answer was no.

15

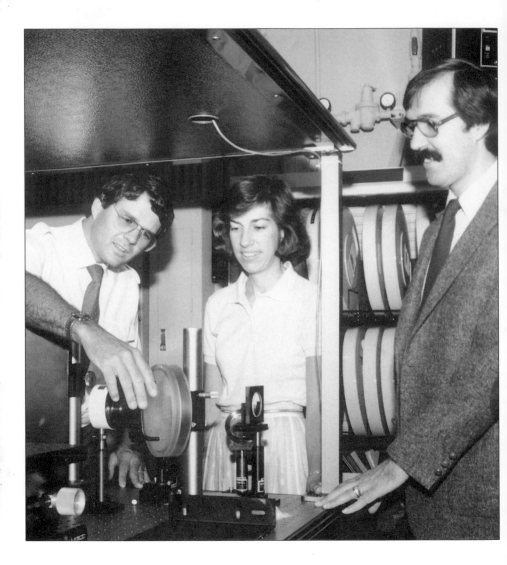

16

Ellen kept trying. She worked hard while she waited for her chance to be an astronaut.

She helped invent new things. She also learned to fly a plane.

Ellen got a job at a space research center. Then in 1990, she got her chance to be an astronaut.

Astronaut training was hard
work. Ellen learned how to
work and live in space.

In April 1993, Ellen's dream
came true. She became the
first Hispanic woman to go
into space.

Ellen flew with four other astronauts. They traveled in the Space Shuttle *Discovery*.

Ellen saw Earth from space for the first time!

23

24

Ellen went into space three more times. She went in 1994, 1999, and 2002.

In space, Ellen did experiments to learn about the Sun. She also worked on the International Space Station.

Things floated inside the Space Shuttle. The astronauts floated, too. Ellen slept in a sleeping bag hooked to a wall.

She strapped herself down to exercise, eat, and play her flute.

28

Ellen likes being an astronaut. Today, she tells young people to work hard in school. She knows school will help them be anything they want to be.

Words You Know

Astronaut   flute

International Space Station

space

Space Shuttle *Discovery*

Index

About the Author

After graduating from Brown University, Elizabeth D. Jaffe received her master's degree in early education from Bank Street College of Education. Since then, she has written many nonfiction children's books and educational materials. She is an editor and lives in New York City.

Photo Credits

Photographs © 2004: Grossmont High School: 8; NASA: 28 (Ames Research Center), 3, 31 top (E. Kopan), cover, 4, 7, 11, 12, 15, 18, 19, 20, 23, 24, 27, 30 top right, 30 top left, 30 bottom, 31 bottom; Courtesy of Sandia National Lab: 16.